Table of Contents

Everyone wants to have a sense of accomplishment. That sense of pride that says, "I created this. I made this. I did this."

There's nothing like the satisfaction that goes with getting things done. Crushing your to-do list as the weight of what once stood before you now lies behind you.

What it means to be productive is different for different people, but the feeling is all the same. For one person, creating a powerful presentation and meeting the needs of a boss or client can make them feel amazing. For another, it may mean finally organizing that closet or starting that business.

For you, it may be completely different, but you know the good feeling you get by putting in a productive day.

The Procrastinator's Guide to Productivity
Tameka Riley

The Battle for Productivity

The Procrastinator's Guide to Productivity
Tameka Riley

Productivity gives you a sense of purpose. It satisfies a deep feeling of accomplishment that fosters a happy life of purpose and fulfillment.

Productivity also allows you the freedom to spend more time with your loved ones and less time worrying about the proverbial can you kicked down the road that you'll one day meet again and still haven't done.

If you're looking for the gratifying sense of accomplishment that can come from being productive, this eBook can help you focus on what will get you there.

Productivity is not easy. There will always be something vying for your attention that wants to cause your productivity to falter.

On any given day, you're constantly faced with a thousand distractions that threaten to hinder your creativity and derail your day. These distractions may be personal or work related, but rest assured, they are always there.

On any given day, you're faced with:

- Notifications, texts, and emails
- Phone Calls
- Unexpected visitors
- Other people's emergencies
- Errands
- Chores
- All sorts of pop ups!

Just as you start getting to important matters, your phone dings. It's a new message that you feel like you should probably check; after all, it will only take a second. You look at your phone and, the

The Procrastinator's Guide to Productivity
Tameka Riley

next thing you know, 4 hours have passed. You've been sucked into the black hole of social media and gone down a rabbit hole that has you trading a few minutes at a time to finish this video, respond to that interaction, or read all 157 comments of someone else's argument. An inbox from a stranger you have to check out. A facetime call. Researching that item you were just talking about that showed up in your newsfeed.

Unfortunately, there will be times when you do your best to set aside distractions, and still wind up feeling like you haven't accomplished anything.

You're busy... **but you're not productive.**

You're doing things...

...but you're not getting anything done.

You answer emails, respond to notifications, respond to texts and message make sure nobody feels neglected...

...but still come away each day not accomplishing anything.

Some days you feel like you've worked really hard, but your dreams remain untouched and dusty. Sitting on the shelf you last put them on. You wake up and go to bed exhausted, but you don't have anything to show for it. You know there's more to life, but you just don't know where to start.

In this book, **you'll discover four pillars of productivity.**

These pillars will help you achieve the sense of accomplishment you've been searching for. Instead of ending your day feeling defeated by piles of work undone, you can go to bed with a sense of peace, knowing that you've done enough for the day.

You've done the work and you can be satisfied with what you've accomplished.

Systems Over Goals

The Procrastinator's Guide to Productivity
Tameka Riley

You've probably been told that in order to achieve anything meaningful, you need to turn it into a goal.

Well... perhaps.

While goals can be helpful, they may not always be ideal.

The Problem with Goals

Goals have **a termination point.**

In other words, you're not successful until you've reached your goal, and until you've reached the goal you might feel like:

- You're spinning your wheels, not going anywhere.
- You're a failure.
- You haven't accomplished anything until you've reached a distant finish line

Though unpopular, if this is the only way you measure success, you feel defeated when your goals are loft and ambitious.

For example, if you want to own a major corporation, nothing you do will make you feel like you've succeeded until you reach that goal. No matter how incredible your strides, you'll rarely pat yourself on the back until you've attained it, but how long until you're able to pat yourself on the back?

The Procrastinator's Guide to Productivity
Tameka Riley

Honestly, even when you achieve your goal, you simply have to start all over again with the next one. If you even know what it is. Unless it pales in comparison to your previous goal, how much longer before you attain your next sense of accomplishment?

Even worse, you might feel the temptation to fall back into old habits, because, let's face it, going all the way back to the starting line after accomplishing such a feat is not something most people look forward to. Where do you go once you've finally 'arrived'? Back to the beginning?

The Procrastinator's Guide to Productivity
Tameka Riley

The Power of Systems

There is a better way.

They're called systems. Systems allow you to:

- Make progress on your goals every single day
- Bolster your success by shifting your mindset
- Help you set and reach measurable milestones and celebrate their achievement
- Avoid feeling that you're just spinning your wheels and not going anywhere

What are Systems?

Scott Adams, author of the famous Dilbert cartoons, wrote about systems in his book, How to Fail at Almost Everything and Still Win Big: Kind of the Story of My Life.

He explained the difference between systems and goals like this: "Losing ten pounds may be a goal, while the system is learning to eat right."

For example: Your goal is to clean your house from top to bottom. After an entire day, you're finally satisfied. But without a system in place, your satisfaction is short lived as your home goes right back into disarray the following week.

In a matter of days…

…dishes overwhelm the sink, laundry has piled up again, the floors are a mess and the trash needs to go out.

A system, on the other hand, would be a routine in which you train yourself to do small tasks each day. The result is a house that's tidy, and remains so for more than a few days.

Now let's apply that to business:

- **Goal:** To generate a minimum of $50,000 in revenue in the next two months.

- **System:** Every morning you make a pre-determined number of calls to potential clients and follow up with existing ones for new opportunities.

The Procrastinator's Guide to Productivity
Tameka Riley

Having a system in place helps develop daily habits to ensure you reach your target.

Using a system does not mean that you have no goals. **It simply means that you shift your focus to the process more than the destination.**

So, What's Wrong with Goals?

You've probably always been told to set lofty goals and work hard to achieve them.

On the surface, there's nothing wrong with goals. Goals inspire, motivate, and challenge us. They give us something to strive for. A sense of purpose.

But goals can also be unforgiving.

Let's say you set a goal in your business to make X amount of sales by the end of the year.

You grind, you push your team to do the same. All year long, striving to achieve a certain number.

What happens when you don't reach your number?

Chances are, even if you sell more than you've ever sold in the history of the company...

...you'll still feel like a failure. Barely even taking time to celebrate the records you've broken and the strides you made, because a number someone scratched

The Procrastinator's Guide to Productivity
Tameka Riley

on a piece of paper said it wasn't good enough.

That sense of defeat is even worse than the opportunities you missed to bond and celebrate your many victories along the way. And trust me, they were there.

Bottom line?

Being overly focused on a large, distant goal can give you tunnel vision, and that's not always a good thing.

Tunnel vision on a singular goal may have kept you from taking the time to develop a new product or service that could have been sold for twice as much.

Scott Adams writes:

"...if you focus on one goal, your odds of achieving it are better than if you have no goal. But you also miss out on opportunities that might have been far better than your goal... With a system you are less likely to miss one opportunity because you were too focused on another. With a system, you are always scanning for any opportunity."

Goals Limit Your Threshold for Happiness

One problem with goals is that your view is so narrowly focused on the top of a huge mountain in the distance that you aren't giving yourself permission to enjoy the journey getting there.

The Procrastinator's Guide to Productivity
Tameka Riley

Once you reach a goal:

- Where do you go once the feeling of happiness you waited so long to get to fades?

- You'll then feel the need to achieve the next goal and the next, each with gratification delayed so long it's hard to stay motivated.

- You're continually chasing a singular future event whose gratification is fleeting.

In his book, Atomic Habits, Productivity expert James Clear writes:

"When you fall in love with the process rather than the product, you don't have to wait to give yourself permission to be happy.

The Procrastinator's Guide to Productivity
Tameka Riley

You can be satisfied anytime your system is running. And a system can be successful in many different forms, not just the one you first envision."

What Happens When You Reach Your Goal?

You may realize that once you've achieved a goal, you have nothing left to work towards and no daily systems in place to sustain what you've accomplished.

For example, let's say you set a goal to run a marathon.

In order to achieve this:

- You pressed your way into the gym five days a week.

- You changed your diet and quit eating anything you enjoy.
- You forced yourself to run even though you hated every step.

You worked extremely hard, and hated the very process that got you there.

Once your goal was met, you were so glad it was over you hated the very thought going back to such an arduous regiment.

Soon, you've abandoned the gym, your routine is a thing of the past, and your running shoes are growing mold in the back of your closet.

What went wrong?

You were only focused on the goal, but your system was unbearable.

The Procrastinator's Guide to Productivity
Tameka Riley

So why did you start running in the first place? Maybe because you wanted to be healthier, stronger, feel better.

Scott Adams explains that while you can set a rigid schedule to exercise several times a week, if you're not enjoying the exercise, there's a higher risk that you're going to give it up.

You may do it for a time, once the goal is accomplished, you'll lack the willpower to continue what feels like a punishment.

Instead, he suggests choosing to be active each day to a level that feels good. **In this scenario...**

- You're training yourself that being active is positive.

The Procrastinator's Guide to Productivity
Tameka Riley

- You're receiving a psychological lift from the experience.

- You're training your body and mind to enjoy being active as opposed to hating it.

The desire to challenge yourself as you continue to enjoy being active will come naturally. Though you began with short, slow walks, you may eventually find that you actually like running. No pressure.

Wanting to and forcing yourself to make the difference.

How Do Systems Help?

One of the most important things about systems is that they are much more flexible than goals.

This shift may be a little uncomfortable at first, especially if you have a type A personality. It may even feel as though you're giving up control because you're not focusing so much energy on a distant event in the future.

The big question you may have is: **What happens when you shift your focus from a concrete goal to the process instead?**

Focusing on the system does not mean that you're wandering aimlessly and abandoning your goals.

For example: Suppose a sports coach chooses to focus on developing great plays, picking incredible players, and creating effective practice routines instead of simply winning?

He would still have a winning team, but more the goal is more attainable, the results are more sustainable, and the journey is more enjoyable.

James Clear writes:

> "Every Olympian wants to win a gold medal. Every candidate wants to get the job. And if successful and unsuccessful people share the same goals, then the goal cannot be what differentiates the winners from the losers...The goal had always been there. It was only when they implemented a system of continuous small improvements

The Procrastinator's Guide to Productivity
Tameka Riley

that they achieved a different outcome."

Everyone wants to win, but not everyone does. Why?

In order to be successful in your business, it's important to understand what is and isn't working in your process.

Think about the things in your system that are working and the things that are not.

What does your hiring process look like?

- Do you have strong, loyal employees?

- Do they have a valid understanding of your vision and the direction in which you're heading?

The Procrastinator's Guide to Productivity
Tameka Riley

- If you're away, are they empowered enough to keep your company running like a well-oiled machine or will things fall apart at the seams?

- If you answered "No" to any of these questions, how can you put better systems in place to steer your ship in a better direction?

Let's talk about your marketing campaign and the system that drives it.

- Is it working?

- What changes can you implement to reach more customers in your business?

Now think about the systems you have in place to support your products and services.

The Procrastinator's Guide to Productivity
Tameka Riley

- What are some of your areas of improvement?

- How can you streamline the process to make it more efficient?

- Are your products or services testing well in the marketplace?

- If not, what can you do to improve them?

Small, day-to-day improvements help you feel accomplished and productive. Learning to push through daily struggles brings confidence and happiness in a way that a distant, hard to reach goal never will.

Systems not only teach you how to become better at what you do, they develop your skill level and create daily habits that will sustain the goal once you achieve it.

If you find something isn't working, you have the flexibility to make a quick adjustment and keep it moving.

The Early Bird Gets Things Done

The Procrastinator's Guide to Productivity
Tameka Riley

Most successful people can tell you, there's nothing like the peaceful calm of the early morning hours. The atmosphere is quiet, you're fresh from your night's rest, and you virtually have the place to yourself.

It's one of the best times to tackle your most important tasks before most of the world even wakes up. This thinking is called "mind over mattress" and it's been around for a long time.

You may also be familiar with Benjamin Franklin's quote, "Early to bed and early to rise, makes a man healthy, wealthy, and wise."

There are numerous successful people who subscribe to this belief:

- Apple CEO Tim Cook gets up as early as 3:45 am.

- Michelle Gas, CEO of Kohl's department stores, gets up at 4:30 am to go running.

- Former PepsiCo CEO Indra Nooyi rises at 4:00 am and is in the office by 7:00. In 2012, she told Fortune, "They say sleep is a gift that God gives you...That's one gift I was never given."

- Twitter co-founder, Jack Dorsey, wakes up at 5:30 am to meditate and go for a six-mile jog.

The Procrastinator's Guide to Productivity
Tameka Riley

- Starbucks CEO, Howard Schultz, is up at 4:00 am and in the office by 6:00 am.

- Richard Branson, a businessman behind the Virgin group of companies, rises at 5:45 am for an early morning workout and breakfast.

And there many more examples of these early bird business machines.

What makes early risers successful, and how do you become one?

What Does Science Say?

You may be wondering if this old adage is true. Do early risers really live happier, more productive lives?

Here's what the researchers have to say:

Night Owls are More Prone to Negative Thought Patterns

In 2014, the Department of Psychology at Binghamton University completed a study that included 100 undergraduate students. Their study found that both people who get less sleep, and those who delay sleep, are prone to Repetitive Negative Thinking (RNT).

RNT is a transdiagnostic disorder that can be observed in other disorders such as depression and anxiety. It's correlated with high levels of worry and negative thought patterns.

Early Risers Increase Their Chance of Success

In 2010, Harvard Business Review released a study about early risers by biologist Christoph Randler.

367 university students were asked about the times of the day they were most energetic and willing to take action to change a situation to their advantage.

Randler reported, "A higher percentage of the morning people agreed with statements that indicate proactivity, such as 'I spend time identifying long-range goals for myself' and 'I feel in charge of making things happen.'"

He went on to say:

> "My earlier research showed they tend to get better grades in school, which get them into better colleges, which then lead to better job opportunities. Morning people also anticipate problems and try to minimize them, my survey showed. They're proactive. A number of studies have linked this trait, proactivity, with better job performance, greater career success, and higher wages."

In 2008, Kendry Clay conducted a similar study at the University of North Texas. 824 psychology students were asked about their sleep habits and daytime functions.

The Procrastinator's Guide to Productivity
Tameka Riley

The study found that students who preferred the morning had higher GPAs than those who preferred the evening.

Both studies had the outcome: **Early risers have a much higher chances of success than night owls.**

7 Ways to be an Early Riser

Rising early sounds good, but it's not always so easy. Thankfully, there are things you can do to ditch the bed and jump-start the day.

Tip #1: Change Your Bedtime

One of the easiest ways to get out of bed in the morning is to change your bedtime. I know, duh, right? It sounds obvious, but you would be surprised at the number of people who want to become a morning person, only to spend the night scrolling themselves to sleep in the wee hours of the morning on social media. Consuming content they won't even remember the next day. Go. To. Bed.

There are times where the late evening hours might even feel like a good time to be productive, but **the truth is:**

- You have a limited threshold for productivity.
- Your progress is going to stall.
- Your work is probably going to get sloppy.

The Procrastinator's Guide to Productivity
Tameka Riley

Instead, do your most productive work during the daytime hours when you're fresh and alert. Leave the evening for winding down and enjoying time with family and friends.

Some people are night owls, and trust me, I get it. So was I, but that can be changed. Start by going to bed one hour earlier and getting up and hour earlier for a start and push it back from there. Gradually, your body clock will adjust, and you will find it more productive.

Tip #2: Turn off the Screens

Tablets, laptops, smartphones, televisions; our lives are filled with screens. We're surrounded by them. Integrated into them. From our screens we work, bank, connect with others, do business, control our homes and even start our cars.

These tools are extremely useful and captivating, but when bedtime comes, they can affect not only your sleep, but your relationships in a way we may not have intended.

The National Sleep Foundation says that technology/screens can affect our sleep in three very big ways:

1. **By suppressing melatonin,** the hormone that controls your sleep/wake cycle.

2. **By keeping your brain active.** By keeping your mind engaged with social media, work, or television, you're sending the message to your brain that it's time to stay awake

The Procrastinator's Guide to Productivity
Tameka Riley

and active.

3. **Phone alerts that wake you up through the night.** If you're one who keeps your cell phone on your nightstand, or worse, in bed with you, the sound of emails, texts, and notifications disturb your sleep. No matter how you may try to ignore, your curiosity inevitably gets the best of you and rise up for a peek, taking you completely out of recuperative REM sleep.

An easy way to keep your sleep from being disturbed, turn it off and put it away at least two hours before bedtime. Even better, do not bring it into the bedroom at all. Allow your mind and body to wind down and prepare for a peaceful night's rest.

I understand that some may use their phone as an alarm clock, but this creates an enormous temptation to check emails and social media in an attempt to "scroll yourself to sleep". It will prove much more beneficial to you if you buy yourself an alarm clock and allow our devices to charge in a separate room. Get rid of the nighttime distractions and rest.

Tip #3: Create a Sleep Routine

Sleep routines are common among parents with small children, but it is not limited to children alone. A sleep routine is an excellent way to develop positive habits for getting a good night's rest. **In time, your body will adjust, and you will find that you won't need an alarm clock**

at all.

The National Sleep Foundation suggests:

- Finding a relaxing routine activity away from bright lights

- Trying to avoid activities that can cause excitement or stress

If you feel the need to occupy your thoughts before bed, try reading the bible, or an inspirational book. This is a great way to reduce stress and bring peace to your mind and emotions. According to Cognitive Neuropsychologist Dr. David Lewis, his sleep study found that reading can reduce stress by up to 68%.

Other things that are helpful to include in your nighttime routine are:

- A warm, non-caffeinated drink
- Sleep sounds or apps
- Positive meditation and prayer
- A warm bath
- Deep breathing exercises
- Thoughts of love and gratitude

Tip #4: Get Moving & Exercise

A good workout or simply getting the body moving during the day is a great way to get a good night's rest. It has been found to increase the dept, length and quality of your sleep.

Physical activity is also known to reduce stress and anxiety -- two things that greatly affect your ability to relax enough to fall and stay asleep.

Tip #5: Put Some Distance Between You And Your Alarm Clock

If your struggle is waking up in the morning, put your alarm clock out of reach. Place your alarm clock on the opposite side of the room so when the temptation to hit the snooze button comes, you will be forced out of bed and wide awake by the time you get there.

Tip #6: A Splash of Cold Water

Once you've crossed the room to turn off the alarm, try splashing some cold water on your face to avoid crawling back

The Procrastinator's Guide to Productivity
Tameka Riley

under the covers. The cold water will help energize you and snap you out of grogginess and into the day.

Tip #7: Find Your Reason to Get Up

Try to start your day with something you look forward to.

Everyone's reason may not be the same but try to find a good one. Life is such a gift denied to so many people who pray to be where you are, give yourself a good reason to wake up. Choose something that will be effective every day.

Knowing that you are not yet where you want to be may be enough. The fact that you can be more productive in the morning may be enough. To get a warm fuzzy from your little ones might do it for you. If not, plan a nice breakfast, put your favorite coffee on a timer, find your reason.

Kill Your Distractions

The Procrastinator's Guide to Productivity
Tameka Riley

You know those days. You've planned your day to crush your to-do list. You're going to buckle down this time. You're finally in the right mindset and you're ready to roll.

You're completely geared up to knock it out the park today. You can almost feel that feeling of relief and satisfaction you'll have at the end of the day.

Then... the phone dings -- it's a text.

Your laptop chimes with a Facebook interaction.

Your phone lights up with a 'Make This Go Viral' DM.

A procrastinator reaches out with another "last minute emergency".

The Procrastinator's Guide to Productivity
Tameka Riley

Your phone rings – it's drama and you know it.

You get distracted researching step 4 when you haven't completed step 1.

You need to use the bathroom. A drink of water. A snack. A cup of coffee.

Before you know it, you're in a social media rabbit hole watching a video after getting sidetracked from the interaction that was only going to take a second. Now your entire morning is blown and you have nothing to show for it.

Unfortunately, **distractions are one of the main killers of productivity.** You have so much is coming at you, all threatening to cause you to spin your wheels and keep you from focusing on what really matters.

The Procrastinator's Guide to Productivity
Tameka Riley

While you're busy with distractions, you're accomplishing nothing, and gaining even less.

So how do you eliminate distractions and get to what's really important?

Here's 5 tips for getting rid of distractions and getting back on track.

Tip #1: Plan your day the Night Before

Planning your day the night before can be extremely helpful in keeping you focused on the following day.

You don't have to plan every move and decision, but try to make choices that will keep your day flowing in a particular direction during the day.

For example:

- What you're wearing
- What's for breakfast/lunch
- Defrost what you'll need for dinner
- Plan the way you'll get to work

When you're tired in the morning, these decisions are harder to make and can unnecessarily interrupt your thought processes.

Also, set a rough schedule to determine your direction. For example, you might decide not to check your messages until you've completed two important tasks. Or for the first two hours of the day, you'll focus solely on a specific project.

The Procrastinator's Guide to Productivity
Tameka Riley

Tip #2: Cut Out Social Media

People are spending an estimated 2.5 hours a day on social media. That's great if you're an advertiser, but terrible if you're trying to be productive.

Social media can be great for networking and marketing, but...

- Always giving your opinion and responding to the opinion of others
- Constantly checking notifications
- Scrolling through endless videos
- Comparing yourself with strangers on Instagram
- Checking to see who typed "lol" on your latest post
- Reading all 287 comments in an online argument

…Isn't going to help you be productive.

If you let it, social media can be a black, time sucking hole. It's addictive and entertaining, but if you're not careful, you'll waste entire days doing absolutely nothing.

Occasional use isn't bad. You may catch up with distant relatives, old friends, network, learn new things, find a great group to bolster your business or hobby, etc.

Here are some strategies to help you manage your social media time:

- Set a schedule for – for example, between 10 - 11 a.m. and 4 - 5 p.m.

- Use tools like "Android Digital Wellbeing" and "iOS Screen Time" to monitor or restrict social media use.

- Turn off notifications that aren't business related so you're not distracted by feeling the constant pull of "dings".

Use your social media accounts you've set up for business to engage with customers, post your newest product and images. After that, put your phone away.

Tip #3: Create Boundaries

In any given day, you'll have to field calls, notifications, and messages. Some lines of communication are necessary, but there are others that can be set aside.

Give yourself times during your day when you don't check every notification or message.

Some choose early mornings to return phone calls and messages and engage with others. Others find it more productive to focus on their list of tasks before creating new tasks introduced by outside messages.

Choose what works best for you but find your rhythm and stick to it. It's extremely important to set times when you're not in

The Procrastinator's Guide to Productivity
Tameka Riley

constant contact with outside distractions.

It's also a good idea to leave at least one day a week where you're not scheduled to be anywhere or do anything at all. This gives you a free day of uninterrupted focus stay productive.

Tip #4: Create a Productive Space

If you work from home or in an office space, it's important to create a productive space.

Productivity produces productivity.

In other words, if you were productive in a particular space, your brain will want to be productive there again. You will associate that place with the great feeling you had the last time you were able to crush it.

Likewise, if you have a space you associate with entertainment -- like the living room where the TV is, the dining room where you laugh and fellowship with friends and family -- you'll want to do those fun things whenever you're there.

Try to keep fun places and workplaces separate and make your workspace is conducive for work.

In order for your workplace to promote work, keep it tidy. Clutter will only distract you. Even if you don't feel like you have to clean it up right away, the disorganization will pull on you and cloud your atmosphere.

The Procrastinator's Guide to Productivity
Tameka Riley

Keep it simple and easy to maintain and if you can, make sure it has a door so you can shut out distractions when needed.

Tip #5: It Can't All Be Work

We're not meant to work all the time and never unwind. There are a few unicorns who never take time out to play, but that's certainly not the norm, nor is it recommended.

In his book Play: How It Shapes the Brain, Opens the Imagination, and Invigorates the Soul, Psychiatrist Stuart Brown, the founder of the National Play Institute writes, "The truth is that play seems to be one of the most advanced methods nature has invented to allow a complex brain to create itself."

Play relieves us of heavy workloads and opens sus up for creativity. Some workplaces like Google even have built in areas for play at the office. These spaces relieve stress and foster creativity in the workplace.

Dr. Brown goes on to explain:

> "…there is a kind of magic in play. What might seem like a frivolous or even childish pursuit is ultimately beneficial. It's paradoxical that a little bit of "nonproductive" activity can make one enormously more productive and invigorated in other aspects of life."

Most people get unproductive and frustrated when they force themselves to constantly work without taking time to enjoy themselves. This is a system that is not very sustainable.

Here are a few things you can do to combat this:

1. **Make work fun**. Find ways to make your daily tasks light and fun, as opposed to approaching them with dread and resentment in your heart. This takes a mindset shift. Include a happy tune, dance a little, feign excitement until it runs through you.

2. **Challenge yourself in a contest** in which you may be the only participant. Set a goal and reward yourself when you reach it.

3. **Plan breaks throughout the day.** Take a brisk walk around the block,

take a coffee break or have a good lunch.

- These may seem like distractions, but when coupled with a renewed focus, they are something to press toward, something to look forward to.

4. **Pick a quitting time and stick to it.** Set aside a time of the day when work ends, and don't pick it up again.

- It's important to leisure time so you can bounce back from work and start the next day fresh and anew.

5. **Take a vacation.** Plan certain times of the year to take an uninterrupted

break. Enjoy yourself, your friends, your family, or simply just be. No phones, no emails, nowhere to be. Relax. It's okay.

There's no way to guarantee you're never distracted, but do what you can to limit them as much as possible. Reduce your consumption of social media, movies, and chit chat when you should be working.
Those activities have their time and place. Make a separate time for play, and you'll soon see that your productive periods are a lot more successful.

Slay Your Dragons

The Procrastinator's Guide to Productivity
Tameka Riley

The final pillar we will focus on is prioritizing your day. Starting the day tackling low hanging fruit is easy; but the most productive people focus on getting their most important task done first before adding more things on their plate; usually found in their inbox.

Slay your dragon (hardest task) first.

Mark Twain said, "If it's your job to eat a frog, it's best to do it first thing in the morning. And if it's your job to eat two frogs, it's best to eat the biggest one first."

In other words, before you do anything else, tackle the hardest things first.

What Does the Research Say?

How does this flesh out in real life? Is it practical?

In 2017, Harvard Business School released a working paper called Task Selection and Workload: A Focus on Completing Easy Tasks Hurts Long-Term Performance.

The study was conducted in an emergency department in a metropolitan hospital. They…" assembled [their] data from the emergency department for twenty-four months in fiscal years 2006-2007 involving over 90,000 distinct patient encounters."

The study was meant to reveal how productivity was impacted by starting with easier tasks versus harder ones.

The Procrastinator's Guide to Productivity
Tameka Riley

As revealed in the study, while completing easier tasks does create a short-term sense of satisfaction, it significantly impacts long-term productivity.

The paper goes on to explain:

"By selecting the easier task (exploitation) an individual gets work done quicker – and likely feels good doing it. However, by choosing the harder task (exploration) one creates an opportunity to learn. Although always selecting the harder task may be suboptimal, if one continually chooses the exploitation path then longer-term performance suffers."

The Procrastinator's Guide to Productivity
Tameka Riley

In other words, a short-term victory feels good for a moment, but a person doesn't feel productive until they actually accomplish something.

Whenever you're not pushing yourself to learn and overcome more difficult tasks, you're limiting your growth and potential.

Additionally, the study revealed that physicians who habitually chose the easier tasks first, were, in the long run, less profitable to the hospital.

Put That Plan into Action

Do your best to take on the most difficult task first. Only you can determine what those are for you. Try to hit hose first in thing in the morning when you're at your freshest. Even though they may not take the longest, they'll take more effort. Get them out of the way when you're at your best.

Your ability to focus diminishes ad the day goes on. Your willpower dwindles and you'll tend to avoid more difficult tasks only to put them off until the next day.

Choosing the hardest jobs first allows you to finish the day more satisfied and accomplished, knocking out the easiest tasks as you close your day. That feeling of productivity ends your day on a high note. That feeling of satisfaction carries you through to the next day when you face that day's dragon with a renewed sense of strength and vigor.

The Procrastinator's Guide to Productivity
Tameka Riley

Productivity Is In Your Grasp

The Procrastinator's Guide to Productivity
Tameka Riley

The sweet fruit of productivity is well within your grasp. It's entirely in your control. You can do this!

To recap, the four pillars are actionable items you can start today are:

- **Pillar #1.** Develop a system that works for you. Make it realistic and sustainable, but continue tweaking it as needed for the best results.

- **Pillar #2.** Go to bed and wake up early so you'll be ready for the day while the rest of the world sleeps.

- **Pillar #3.** Cut out the distractions that interfere with your productivity.

- **Pillar #4.** Crush your most difficult tasks first so you can enjoy the fruits of your and glide into your off hours feeling more satisfied and accomplished.

Your new productive lifestyle will help you live that happy and fulfilled life that you thought was just out of reach.

At the end of the day, you can rest easy knowing that you gave your best effort and put in a productive and fruitful workday. You can put your work aside and invest in the relationships in your life that are most meaningful.

Let's do this!